Wedding Etiquette

Antonia Swinson

Wedding Etiquette

RYLAND
PETERS
& SMALL
LONDON NEW YORK

Designer Sarah Walden
Commissioning Editor Annabel Morgan
Picture Researcher Emily Westlake
Production Patricia Harrington
Art Director Gabriella Le Grazie
Publishing Director Alison Starling

First published in the United Kingdom
in 2003
by Ryland Peters & Small
Kirkman House
12–14 Whitfield Street
London W1T 2RP
www.rylandpeters.com
Text, design and photographs
© Ryland Peters & Small 2003
10 9 8 7 6 5 4 3 2

Printed and bound in China

ISBN 1 84172 511 0

contents

introduction

How should you word your wedding invitations? Who sits at the top table? Can the bride make a speech at the reception? All these important questions and many, many more are answered in this beautiful and useful little guide to modern wedding etiquette.

Each section takes a closer look at different elements of a wedding. **People** provides the lowdown on the roles and responsibilities of the members of the wedding party and **Guests** tells you all you need to know on the subject of invitations and gift lists. **Money** covers the tricky subject of who pays for what. The practicalities of flowers, transport and the wedding processional are discussed in **The Ceremony**, while **The Reception** takes a look at the etiquette of the seating plan, the speeches and the cutting of the cake.

This little book aims to be a friendly guide, leading you through the maze of wedding etiquette by providing advice on when it's best to stick to tradition...and when it's fine to break the rules!

wedding customs and traditions

♡ White weddings were an invention of the Victorians. Before then brides simply wore their best dress to get married in, sometimes with a white ribbon attached to symbolize purity.

♥ Veils were thought to keep away evil spirits, who would be confused by not being able to see the bride.

♡ Chimney sweeps are associated with the hearth and home, and it's thought to be good luck to kiss one on the way to the ceremony.

♥ The wedding ring symbolizes everlasting love. It's thought that the ancient Egyptians started the practice of wearing one on the third finger of the left hand – they believed that the vein in that finger ran straight to the heart.

♡ Throwing confetti has its roots in the Roman period, when guests threw almonds at newlyweds to symbolize a fruitful marriage.

♥ Cutting a cake at a wedding was once thought to ensure a fruitful marriage. Keeping a piece of cake is supposed to guarantee that your husband stays faithful.

♡ The honeymoon gets its name from the tradition of newlyweds drinking honeyed mead (a symbol of life and fertility) until the waning of the moon.

♥ Wedding receptions have their roots in the medieval period, when the groom had to demonstrate that he could support his wife by giving gifts of food and drink to his in-laws.

♡ Bouquets were originally posies of herbs, carried to ward off evil spirits.

Something old,
something new,
something borrowed,
something blue,
and a silver sixpence in your shoe.

This verse refers to the bride's passage from her old life to her new one. 'Something borrowed' means that marriage involves sharing; 'something blue' alludes to the colour's association with constancy; 'and a silver sixpence in your shoe' refers to the hope of prosperity in marriage.

People

On the big day, the bride and groom are undoubtedly the stars of the show, but their best man, attendants and ushers play very important supporting roles.

attendants and helpers

The helpers There are no hard and fast rules about attendants – whether or not you have bridesmaids and ushers is purely a matter of personal choice. If you're having a register office wedding, you may not need ushers for the ceremony. It's usual to have a best man – some people even have two – and the best man could even be a best woman. There's a lot to think about when you're organizing a wedding, so if you do have attendants, make use of your chief bridesmaid and best man when you need extra help before the day.

Attendants The bride may want to have a chief bridesmaid (she's called this if she's single, and matron of honour if she's married). The chief bridesmaid is the bride's right-hand woman on the day, so she should be well-organized and practical. If there isn't a chief bridesmaid, parcel out her duties (see next page) among your adult bridesmaids. There's no doubt that young bridesmaids (also known as flower girls) and pageboys add great charm to a wedding, but it can be a long and tiring day for them. The best man is the groom's chief helper and has a fairly long list of duties and a speech to make. He also needs to be organized and calm.

female members of the bridal party

Chief bridesmaid

Her duties are:

- ♥ To organize the hen party.
- ♡ To help the bride get ready before the wedding.
- ♥ To make sure that the bride's honeymoon luggage is sent to the reception venue or on to the hotel.
- ♡ To wait for the bride to arrive outside the ceremony venue and keep an eye on any young attendants.
- ♥ To arrange the bride's veil and train before she walks down the aisle.
- ♡ To take the bride's bouquet at the top of the aisle and look after it during the ceremony. She returns the bouquet to the bride for her walk back down the aisle.
- ♥ To look after the bride's dress once she's changed into her going-away outfit.

The bride's mother Traditionally, the bride's mother organizes the reception. Her duties include compiling the guest list, sending out invitations, organizing the flowers, ordering or making the cake, booking the photographer and arranging accommodation for the guests. Nowadays, the bride or bridal couple assume many of these duties themselves. On the big day, the bride's mother usually helps dress the bride, supervises young bridesmaids, is present at the signing of the register and may participate in the processional and recessional.

male members of the bridal party

The best man is the groom's chief helper. His duties are:
- ♡ To arrange the stag party.
- ♥ To help organize outfits for himself, the groom and the ushers and to make sure they're collected.
- ♡ To help the groom get ready and get him to the ceremony.
- ♥ To coordinate and direct the ushers.
- ♡ To check that the buttonholes arrive and that the orders of service are ready to be handed out.
- ♥ To look after the ring(s) and hand them to the minister or groom during the ceremony.
- ♡ To make sure that any fees payable on the day are settled.
- ♥ To announce the speeches and the cake-cutting.
- ♡ To read out cards or messages at the reception and make the final speech.
- ♥ To announce the bride and groom's departure from the reception.

Ushers help everything run smoothly on the wedding day. The ushers' duties are:
- ♡ To hand out orders of service as guests arrive and to show them to their seats.
- ♥ To escort the bride's mother and groom's parents to their seats at the front of the church.
- ♡ To seat any latecomers.
- ♥ To get guests together for formal photographs.

Guests

Sharing your day with friends and family, whether it's a select few or a small army of them, will heighten the joy of your celebrations.

the guest list

♥ The size of your guest list is dictated by your budget. If you've set your heart on a certain venue, this may also limit numbers. Once you've set a maximum head count, don't be tempted to exceed it. Don't rely on a drop-out rate, either, because you'll be in trouble if all your guests accept.

♡ The easiest way to draw up a list is to start by including everyone you'd like to invite, then start eliminating names. This is a difficult process, but start by dropping people you haven't seen for several years. You're not obliged to invite colleagues from work or an escort for single friends. Most couples draw up their guest list with their parents. Even if the couple themselves or the bride's parents are footing the whole bill, it's only fair that everyone has a chance to say whom they'd like to invite.

♥ Deciding how to share out the list between the different parties demands diplomacy. Things can be difficult if parents feel their share of the guest list should be larger than the bride and groom would like. There may be distant relatives they want to invite for etiquette's sake, while you would rather invite more friends. Some couples have a two-tiered reception, inviting a small group of guests to the ceremony and meal, then having an evening party to which additional guests are invited.

♡ Remember that if you invite someone to your wedding, it should be because you really want them to be there, so you and your fiancé should have the final say.

inviting children – yes or no

♥ Whether or not to invite children is a tricky decision. There are no rules of etiquette about whether or not to invite them – it depends on your own preference. Some people feel a wedding would not be complete without kids around, while others see it as an adult occasion.

♡ If you decide not to include children, it's diplomatic to let people know verbally, so that you can explain your reasons and avoid causing offence. Bear in mind that some guests won't be able to find babysitters for their children during your wedding and therefore won't be able to come.

♥ Whatever you decide, one decision must go for all. The only exception to this is your immediate family – it's natural to invite little nieces and nephews even if you're not having any other children.

♡ If you do include children, think about ways to keep them happy. If there are lots of them, hire an entertainer or a bouncy castle. A special children's table at the reception is a good idea, complete with crayons and paper or toys and child-friendly food. There are also companies that provide crèche services for weddings.

invitations

♥ Traditional invitations are printed in black on white or cream card and may be hand engraved (the most expensive option), thermographed (looks like hand engraving, but cheaper) or flat printed (the cheapest method). Traditional wordings are given on pages 28–29, but there's no reason why you shouldn't have something less formal if it suits the mood of your wedding.

♡ With formal invitations, guests' names are handwritten in the top left corner or the space provided in the wording of the invitation, and full titles are used. If you're sending an invitation to a married couple, the correct form of address on the envelope is 'Mr and Mrs Joseph Bloggs'.

♥ It's good etiquette to send an invitation to the groom's parents and, if you're having a church wedding, to the minister. If your reception includes a formal dinner and dance and you want guests to wear black tie and evening dress, 'Black Tie' should be printed in the bottom right corner of your invitations. If you're having an evening party to which you're inviting extra guests, there should be a separate invitation for this. It's not considered appropriate to stipulate morning dress on invitations since this could put your guests to inconvenience and expense.

♡ Send invitations out two or three months before the day to be safe, and certainly no later than six weeks before.

wordings for invitations

Here are some standard and alternative wordings for wedding invitations. If you're hosting your own wedding, begin 'Jane Porter and David Broadbent request the pleasure of your company at their marriage...'

invitation to a wedding, bride's parents as hosts:

Mr and Mrs Frederick Porter
request the pleasure of
your company at the marriage
of their daughter
Jane Frances
to
Mr David Broadbent
at St Michael's Church, Wilbury,
on Saturday, 26th July 2003
at 3pm
and afterwards at
The White Swan Hotel, Wilbury

invitation to a wedding, bride's parents as hosts (alternative wording):

Mr and Mrs Frederick Porter
request the pleasure of the company of
[name of guest(s) written by hand]
at the marriage of their daughter
Jane Frances
to
Mr David Broadbent
at St Michael's Church, Wilbury,
on Saturday, 26th July 2003
at 3pm
and afterwards at
The White Swan Hotel, Wilbury

invitation to a wedding, bride's parents divorced and mother remarried:

Mr Frederick Porter and Mrs James Culver
request the pleasure of

If mother is not remarried, begin:

Mr Frederick Porter and Mrs Judy Porter

invitation to a service of blessing:

Mr and Mrs Frederick Porter
request the pleasure of
your company
at the blessing of the marriage
of their daughter
Jane Frances...

invitation to a wedding reception only:

Mr and Mrs Frederick Porter
request the pleasure of
your company at a reception
following the marriage
of their daughter
Jane Frances...

invitation to an evening party only:

Mr and Mrs Frederick Porter
request the pleasure of
your company at an evening party
following the marriage
of their daughter
Jane Frances...

───────────── ♡ ─────────────

invitation to a civil wedding at a licensed venue:

Mr and Mrs Frederick Porter
request the pleasure of
your company at the marriage
of their daughter
Jane Frances
to
Mr David Broadbent
at The White Swan Hotel, Wilbury,
on Saturday, 26th July 2003
at 3pm
followed by a reception

other items of wedding stationery

Place cards If you're having a seating plan at your reception, you'll need place cards for the tables. These can be printed or handwritten.

Reply cards You don't have to include pre-printed reply cards and addressed envelopes with your invitations, though they may encourage guests to reply promptly.

Rachel

Menus These are optional. Your hotel or caterer may be able to supply them, so ask before you order printed ones.

Table plans You'll need one of these if you're having a seated meal, well displayed so guests can easily see where to sit.

Table stationery You may want to go the whole hog and order coasters, napkins, match books and so on with your names or initials and the date of your wedding.

Thank-yous You must take the trouble of handwriting a personal thank-you for any gifts. Tackle them as presents arrive.

Orders of service These contain details of the order of service, music and readings to make it easy for everyone to follow.

the wedding gift list

♥ A gift list serves a practical purpose, saving you from ten-toasters syndrome. It also makes life easy for your guests, who can be confident they've bought you something you really want.

♡ On the other hand, it's important that you don't appear to be greedy or asking for presents. Although many stores provide cards detailing where a list is held to be enclosed with the wedding invitations, it is not considered good etiquette to do so. However, many people do so nowadays.

♥ More and more companies are offering a gift list service, from department stores to specialist shops (and there's nothing to stop you having a list at more than one place). There are also gift list companies which deal with a wide range of suppliers, giving you an enormous choice of products and brands.

♡ A gift list used to help couples to set up home and consisted of household basics – bed linen, china, glassware and so on. However, if you live together already or have been married before, these basics are probably redundant. You may therefore want decorative items for your home or garden, or something special, such as wine or books. If you want to put expensive items on your list, some stores allow guests to buy part of a gift. You may also be able to put gift vouchers on your list. However, it's not good etiquette to ask for money.

Gift list do's and don'ts

♥ Set up your list well before your wedding so that it's complete by the time your invitations are sent out.

♡ Going round a shop taking endless decisions can be exhausting, so split it up into a couple of trips if necessary.

♥ Make sure your list covers a broad price range.

♡ Don't make your list too long or you'll end up with incomplete sets.

♥ Check the availability of items – there's nothing worse than finding that your dinner service is about to be discontinued.

♡ Write your thank-yous as presents arrive, to save you a mountain of letters after your honeymoon. Letters should be personal and handwritten.

♥ Some guests will bring presents on the day. Ask one of the bridesmaids or ushers to make sure they're safe and that cards are firmly stuck on presents (give them a roll of tape). Someone (perhaps the bride's parents) will have to take home the presents at the end of the reception.

Money

Traditionally, the bride's parents organized and paid for everything to do with the wedding. Nowadays it's more common for both sets of parents to contribute or even for couples to pay for everything themselves.

the budget

♥ Work out who will pay for what and make sure that everyone is clear about what has been decided. Bear in mind that if someone is paying for something, they may feel that it gives them a say in how the money is spent. Be realistic about money: a wedding that's going to leave you financially compromised isn't a good start to married life.

♡ Most couples allocate their biggest chunk of money – around 50 per cent – to the reception. The other main areas, namely wedding clothes and accessories, music, photography, flowers, and other miscellaneous items (invitations, favours and so on), will probably account for about 10 per cent each.

♥ Once you've set a budget, stick to it. Add a safety net for unforeseen costs. Get a couple of quotes for every service and remember that, to get an accurate figure, you must provide as much information as possible, especially the number of guests. Read all quotes carefully, including the small print. Watch out for hidden extras such as delivery costs or charges for extra staff. Make sure that all subsequent dealings with your suppliers are in writing and check when they need to know final numbers. File all your quotes and bills as they come in. Keep a running total so you know how on or off target you are.

♡ You'll almost certainly have to pay a deposit when you accept a quote. The balance will be due around the time of the wedding. Check whether you need to arrange for payments to be made while you are away on honeymoon.

who pays for what

Below is the traditional breakdown of who pays for what.
Nowadays the bridal couple and both sets of parents often
share wedding costs.

The bride's parents
♡ wedding stationery
♥ the bride's outfit and accessories
♡ the flowers for the ceremony and reception
♥ the music for the ceremony and reception
♡ the photographer and videographer
♥ the transport
♡ the reception, including food and drink
♥ the cake

The groom
♡ the bride's engagement and wedding rings
♥ bouquets for the bride and her attendants, corsages and
buttonholes
♡ all ceremony or church fees (including organist and choir)
♥ presents for the attendants, best man and ushers
♡ the first-night hotel
♥ the honeymoon

The bride
♡ the groom's wedding ring

The Ceremony

Whether you exchange your vows
in a church, synagogue or licensed
venue, the marriage ceremony is
at the heart of the day. Then the
celebrations can begin.

flowers

The bride's bouquet There's no rule to say that the bride must carry a bouquet, but most do, as flowers add a decorative touch and give the nervous bride something to do with her hands. Etiquette says that the bride should not carry flowers if she opts to wear a hat instead of a veil, but like many old-fashioned wedding customs, this one is made to be broken! Traditionally, the bride throws her bouquet as she leaves the reception. The catcher of the bouquet will supposedly be the next to marry.

Buttonholes are usually worn by the bridegroom, best man, ushers and fathers of the couple. Traditionally, they are worn on the left lapel. Make sure buttonholes are securely fastened – an usher should carry extra pins in case of emergency.

Corsages may be worn by the mothers and grandmothers of the couple. Corsages are pinned on to the outfit, usually on the shoulder, lapel or wrist. With clothes made of fine fabric, the corsage should be small and light so it doesn't drag or tear.

Confetti Check with your wedding venue that they're happy for your guests to throw confetti. Paper confetti is available in many shapes and colours, but there are alternatives. Try dried or fresh flower petals or bottles of soap bubbles for guests to blow at you.

transport

♡ The groom and best man normally travel to the ceremony under their own steam, while the bride is treated to something special that then takes the newlyweds to their reception.

♥ The bride and her father (or whoever is giving her away) travel together. The mother of the bride and the bridesmaids travel in the same car (or two, if they can't all fit in one). They leave for the ceremony before the bride and her father.

♡ Travelling to your wedding in a vintage car or horse-drawn carriage is far from essential, but it's one of the things that makes the day fun and special. Any car can be smartened up with a wash and polish and the addition of ribbons or flowers. Alternatives to a carriage or vintage car include modern limousines, white and black taxis and sports cars.

Transport tips

♥ Think about practicalities such as the time of year and the weather – important considerations if you want an open carriage – and your dress, which may take up a fair bit of room.

♡ Book as far ahead of your wedding as possible to be sure of getting what you want.

♥ Visit companies to check their vehicles are well maintained.

♡ Get a written estimate – check whether charges are by the hour or are at a set rate, and how much mileage is included. Ask whether your transport will be decorated and if chauffeurs or coachmen will be in uniform.

♥ If you're booking an old car, ask what happens if it breaks down. Will an alternative be available?

the processional and recessional

♥ There is no legal requirement that the bride be given away, either by her father or by anyone else. She can walk down the aisle alone, if she wishes, or even be accompanied by her groom. As wedding traditions become increasingly open to reinterpretation, more and more brides are choosing to ask mothers, siblings or step-parents to give them away. At Jewish weddings, the bride is escorted by both her parents – a tradition that some non-Jewish brides are beginning to adopt.

♡ Traditionally, the bride walks down the aisle on the right arm of her father (or whoever else is giving her away), followed by her attendants – usually the chief bridesmaid first, followed by any other bridesmaids, then the flowergirls and pageboys. The bridegroom and best man wait at the top of the aisle to take their places on the bride's right. The bride hands her bouquet to her chief bridesmaid (or mother) for the duration of the service.

♥ After the ceremony, the bride and groom (with the bride on the groom's left), followed by the attendants, the chief bridesmaid and best man, the bride's mother and groom's father, and the groom's mother and bride's father, process down the aisle.

The Reception

The reception offers a chance to celebrate after the solemnity of the ceremony and the marriage vows. There are few hard and fast rules about how things should be done, so it's up to you whether or not you observe tradition.

reception timetable

♡ The bride and groom should arrive first at the reception, then
the bridesmaids, best man and both sets of parents.

♥ A traditional receiving line is a way of welcoming your guests
personally. The usual order is: bride's mother and father, groom's
mother and father, bride, groom, chief bridesmaid and best man.
If step-parents are involved, it's up to you whether to include them. If
you don't want a formal receiving line, just you and your groom could
welcome people. With lots of guests, a receiving line can be lengthy.

♡ The meal. This can be a sit-down meal or a buffet.

♥ The speeches and toasts (see page 56). Traditionally, these take
place after the meal, but nowadays some couples choose to have
their speeches before, so the bride's father, the groom and the best
man can relax and enjoy their meal.

♡ The cutting of the cake (see page 60).

♥ Receptions often go on into the evening with a dance after the
speeches and cake, or after a short break.

♡ The departure of the bride and groom.

the seating plan

♥ If you're having an informal buffet, you may want your guests to sit wherever they want. For a sit-down meal, a seating plan is a good idea, as it avoids a scramble for places.

♡ Your aim is to put together people who'll enjoy each other's company. Some guests will already know each other. Otherwise, bear in mind a few guidelines. People of the same age are usually best together. Look for things that guests have in common: their children, their jobs and their interests.

♥ Try for a mixture of extroverts and those who need drawing out, and for a balance of men and women. Work single people into the plan early on so you don't use them as 'fillers'.

♡ Married couples should be on the same table, but not next to each other. It's considered polite to place close family and older friends on tables close to the top table.

♥ The bride and groom usually take their seats last so that everyone can applaud them as they come in. The top table is also normally served with food first.

| chief bridesmaid | groom's father | bride's mother | groom | bride | bride's father | groom's mother | best man |

Traditional top table seating plan

The seating plan itself is usually displayed at the entrance to the reception. The plan can be a printed list or you may want to make it into a feature, having it handwritten or decorated in some way. Another approach is to write guests' names and table numbers on little cards, with or without envelopes, and place these on a table for people to collect as they enter.

The top table This is traditionally for the wedding party only, including the bride and groom, both sets of parents, the best man and the chief bridesmaid.

♡ If your and/or your fiancé's parents are divorced and remarried, you'll have to decide whether you want step-parents seated on the top table.

♥ If one parent has remarried but the other has not, it's an idea to find an escort for the unmarried one to balance the table. Perhaps a son or daughter or brother or sister could fit in.

♡ Remember that you and your fiancé's parents should be either side of you as on the traditional plan, with step-parents added on to either end, alternating between men and women.

step-father	chief bridesmaid	groom's father	bride's mother	groom	bride	bride's father	groom's mother	best man	step-mother

Alternative top table seating plan (with step-parents)

the speeches and toasts

♥ There can be few grooms, fathers or best men who positively look forward to giving their speech. However, speeches are an important part of a wedding and provide an opportunity to voice the thoughts and emotions which the day gives rise to.

♡ The traditional order of speeches is as follows: the bride's father (or whoever gave her away); the groom; then the best man.

♥ Nowadays, more and more brides and/or chief bridesmaids are opting to speak too. They can be slotted in wherever seems appropriate, but make sure all the speeches don't run on for too long – try to keep them to 30 minutes in their entirety.

Delivering a speech is always nerve-racking. Here are ten steps to a flawless performance:

♥ Keep to the point – five to ten minutes at most.

♡ Look up, smile and look round at the guests. If you look happy and confident, you'll probably sound it, too.

♥ If you're not naturally witty, don't try too hard. Be sincere and speak from the heart.

♡ Prepare well in advance – not the night before.

♥ Practise your speech out loud a few times and time it to make sure it doesn't overrun. If possible, read it to someone whose opinion you trust.

♡ If you're an inexperienced speaker, write the speech out in full rather than in note form.

♥ Be funny if you can, but avoid sexual innuendoes or anything risqué. Elderly relatives will be listening as well as your friends, so it must be suitable for all.

♡ Keep your sentences short and your language conversational and informal.

♥ If you're not used to speaking in public, use a microphone if there is one. If not, lift your head and project your voice – don't talk into your notes. You'll need to speak up to be heard at the back of the room.

♡ Don't rush, or you'll fall over your words. Take a deep breath and take your time.

who speaks and what they should say

The bride's father
His speech focuses on his daughter. He should say:

♥ How pleased he is to see so many family members and friends at the wedding.

♡ How proud he is of his daughter (he may want to recount some stories from her childhood).

♥ How happy he is to welcome his new son-in-law into the family.

♡ He finishes with a toast to 'the bride and groom'.

The groom
He follows on from and answers the bride's father, thanking him for the toast (he usually manages to get in a mention of his 'wife', which is guaranteed to prompt applause!). His main duty is thanking people:

♥ Everyone who's come to the wedding.

♡ Everyone who's helped to organize the wedding, such as both sets of parents (and anyone else who's contributed financially or otherwise).

♥ His parents for all their help and support over the years (here, he may give a gift or bouquet to his and the bride's mother).

♡ His best man.

♥ His wife for marrying him and being such a beautiful bride.

♡ The attendants for doing such a good job.

♥ He finishes by toasting 'absent friends', then 'the bridesmaids' (and/or pageboys).

The best man
He has a real challenge, as he is expected to be funny. His speech should be tasteful, inspirational and short, avoiding anything smutty or embarrassing. In addition, he should:
♥ Thank the groom for his words and his toast to the attendants.
♡ Read out any messages or cards from absent friends.
♥ Recount some amusing anecdotes about the groom.
♡ Talk about the bride and say what a good couple she and the groom make.
♥ He finishes by toasting 'Mr and Mrs...' and announcing the cutting of the cake.

the cake

The traditional order of events is for cake-cutting to follow the speeches, when everyone's eyes are on the couple. However, nowadays, catering staff often encourage couples to cut the cake before the speeches so that they can take it away and prepare it to be served with coffee afterwards.

♥ The classic wedding cake is a rich fruit mixture, made into three tiers (normally supported by little columns, though it's also popular now to have them stacked) and covered with marzipan and white royal icing.

♡ Fruit cake keeps well and couples often follow the custom of preserving the top tier for the christening of their first child. If you want to do this, remove the icing and marzipan, wrap the cake in greaseproof paper and store in a cool, dark place.

♥ It's a nice idea to send small pieces of cake to people who can't attend the wedding.

Alternative ideas for wedding cake

♥ Chocolate, lemon, coffee or carrot cake, or plain Madeira. Remember that if you want an iced cake, the cake itself must be fairly firm so as not to collapse.

♡ French croquembouche, a spectacular pyramid of cream-filled choux-pastry buns topped with caramel or spun sugar. If you want one, find an expert to make it – croquembouche is difficult to make and has to be served very fresh.

♥ Ice-cream cake, pavlova, cheesecake or, to follow one sweet-toothed bride's example, three huge banoffee pies on a tiered cake stand.

♡ A miniature wedding cake for each guest (most practical for small weddings) or individual sponges served with a fruit coulis, crème anglaise or chocolate sauce in place of dessert.

♥ Individual cupcakes or tarts, topped with icing, crystallized flowers or berries.

Decoration

The inspiration for your cake could come from any number of sources: you and your fiancé's shared interests; your wedding venue; the time of year; or the flowers and colours you are using. You could have a novelty cake, made to look like a pile of wedding presents, for instance, a giant heart or bow, or perhaps an open book of love poetry.

useful addresses

Wedding websites

www.confetti.co.uk
Very comprehensive
wedding website with
section devoted especially
to wedding etiquette.

www.bride2b.co.uk
This website offers a
directory of suppliers,
help and advice and a
wedding shop specializing
in accessories from
cameras to confetti.

www.foreverafter.co.uk
A glossy online magazine
with lots of useful
information and a UK
supplier directory.

www.hitched.co.uk
Comprehensive site with
information on planning,
venues and bridalwear.

www.net-wedding.co.uk
Another website with an
etiquette section.

www.scottishweddings.co.uk
An online directory of
wedding services north of
the border.

www.webwedding.co.uk
General wedding website
with etiquette and planning
section.

www.weddingflorist.co.uk
Useful nationwide directory
of florists who offer wedding
services, with links to their
websites where applicable.

www.weddingguide.co.uk
Includes a national
wedding directory as well
as lots of practical
information and online
discussions.

www.weddingpages.co.uk
A-Z directory providing
information on local
wedding services
nationwide.

www.weddings.co.uk
Section on wedding
customs and superstitions
as well as an online
wedding diary.

picture credits

Key a= above, b=below, l=left, r=right, c=centre

Polly Wreford
Pages 1, 6-7, 9-11, 22, 23, 28-29, 30-31, 33l, 33ar, 33acr, 34bl, 34br, 36, 39l all, 43br, 48a, 48br, 52l, 52cr, 52br, 56, 57, 60 background, 60 inset above, 62, 63, endpapers

Caroline Arber
Pages 8, 12bc, 12br, 15ar, 15c, 15br, 18l, 18ar, 20b all, 24l all, 26, 27, 33bcr, 34a, 40b all, 43ar, 44, 45, 46, 47, 48bc, 50al, 50ar, 50b, 51, 64cr, 64r

Dan Duchars
15l, 16a, 18cr, 18br, 20a, 33br, 37, 40a, 41, 43l, 50ac, 64cl

Viv Yeo
Pages 12a, 12bl, 13, 21, 24r, 25, 59l, 59r, 64 l

Craig Fordham
Pages 2-3, 5, 15bc, 16b, 17, 35, 39r

David Brittain
Pages 4, 48bl, 49, 52ar, 55, 61,

Peter Cassidy
Pages 32, 34bc, 58, 59c

Sandra Lane
Page 60 inset below

acknowledgments

The publisher would like to thank everyone who made
the photography for this book possible. Special thanks go
to the brides and grooms: Annabel and David, Catherine
and Scott, Lizzie and Justin, and Berenice and Jamie
for so graciously allowing us to photograph their
beautiful weddings. Thanks also to our beautiful little
'bridesmaids': Arianna, Niamh, Rita, Shannon and Stella.